Neighborhood Walk

City

Peggy Pancella

Heinemann Library
Chicago, Illinois

© 2006 Heinemann Library
a division of Reed Elsevier Inc.
Chicago, Illinois

Customer Service   888–454–2279

Visit our website at www.heinemannlibrary.com

Photo research by Jill Birschbach
Designed by Joanna Hinton-Malivoire and Q2A Creative
Printed in China by South China Printing Co.

10 09 08 07 06
10 9 8 7 6 5 4 3 2 1

Library of Congress Cataloging-in-Publication Data
Pancella, Peggy.
  City / Peggy Pancella.
     p. cm. -- (Neighborhood walk)
  Includes bibliographical references and index.
  ISBN 1-4034-6215-1 (hc) -- ISBN 1-4034-6221-6 (pb)
  1. Cities and towns--Juvenile literature. 2. City and town life--Juvenile literature. I. Title. II. Series.
  HT152.P36 2006
  307.76--dc22

                        2005010647

Acknowledgments
The author and publisher are grateful to the following for permission to reproduce copyright material:
Corbis pp. **4** (right), **6**, **14**, **25**; Getty Images pp. **5** (bottom, Photodisc/Jeremy Woodhouse), **5** (top, Photodisc/McDaniel Woolf), **7** (Donovan Reese), **9** (Photolink/Photodisc), **10** (Photolink/Photodisc), **15** (Jeremy Hoare), **24** (Larry Brownstein); Heinemann Library pp. **4** (left, Robert Lifson), **8** (Jill Birschbach), **11** (Brian Warling), **13** (Jill Birschbach), **16** (Robert Lifson), **17** (Robert Lifson), **18** (Greg Williams), **19** (Robert Lifson), **20** (Robert Lifson), **21** (Brian Warling), **26** (Robert Lifson), **27** (Robert Lifson), **29** (Robert Lifson); Photo Edit, Inc. **12** (Rudi Von Briel), **22** (Barbara Stitzer), **23** (Mary Kate Denny), **28** (Tony Freeman)

Cover photograph reproduced with permission of Getty Images (Taxi/Ron Chapple)

Some words are shown in bold, **like this**. You can find out what they mean by looking in the glossary.

Contents

Let's Visit a City

People everywhere live in **neighborhoods**.
A neighborhood is a small part of a larger
community, such as a city or town.
A neighborhood's people and places help
to make it special.

Some neighborhoods are parts of cities. A city is a very large community. It may have thousands or even millions of people. A city and the communities around it make up a **metropolitan area**.

Homes

People live in all parts of a city. **Downtown,** most people live in apartments. Sometimes, apartments are built in old factories and office buildings.

Some apartment buildings are very tall.

These town houses are all connected to each other.

Outside the downtown, the city is divided into many **neighborhoods**. People live in houses, apartment buildings, or **town houses**. The homes in each neighborhood are often alike in some ways.

Getting Around

Buses take people around the city.

In cities, some people use cars to get from place to place. But city streets are often very busy and crowded. Some people choose to walk or ride bikes. Others use buses or taxis.

People come into the city to work, shop, or attend special events. They may ride on buses, trains, or **subways**. Some people **carpool** to save money.

Trains can carry many people at one time.

Schools

Cities have many children, so they need many schools. Most **neighborhoods** have at least one school. There are schools **downtown** as well.

Schools in cities need to have room for lots of students.

Children in city schools enjoy playing outdoors.

City school buildings are often quite large. Most of them have play areas nearby. Some children can walk to their neighborhood school. Others ride bikes or in cars, school buses, city buses, or **subways**.

Working

Many people work **downtown**. Here, there are large office buildings and **government** buildings. There are stores, restaurants, factories, and other businesses, too.

Cities are full of people who work.

Repair workers
help make a
city safe.

Workers in the city do many different kinds
of jobs. Some work in offices, restaurants, or
stores. Others build and repair the roads
and buildings that the city needs.

Keeping Safe

Police officers are
always ready
to help.

Many workers help keep the city safe. Some
police officers **patrol** the city in cars. Others
walk or ride bikes or horses. This helps them get
around traffic more easily.

Firefighters and **emergency** workers also keep people in a city safe. They rush to help when people are hurt, sick, or in danger. Their quick work can save people's lives.

Ambulances sometimes rush people to a hospital.

Shopping

Cities have many different places to shop. There are large **department stores** that sell all kinds of things. There are other stores that sell special products.

Department stores in cities can be very tall.

People can walk from shop to shop to buy different things.

City **neighborhoods** have many places to shop, too. These stores are usually smaller and sell special kinds of products. Sometimes stores are grouped together in a certain area.

Food

Everyone needs food to eat. Most people in cities get their food from grocery stores. Large grocery stores sell many kinds of food. Some **neighborhoods** also have smaller stores and **farmers' markets**.

Large city grocery stores sell many kinds of food.

People sometimes enjoy eating outdoors on nice days.

Cities have many places to eat. There are fast food restaurants and sidewalk **cafés**. Some restaurants serve foods from different countries. Sometimes you can even buy food from **vendors** on the streets.

19

Libraries

A big city needs many libraries. There is often a main library **downtown**. People can borrow books and look up information. They can also join book clubs or use computers.

Most cities have a large main library downtown.

Some libraries have music to listen to or videos to watch.

Many city **neighborhoods** have smaller **branch** libraries. Branch libraries share books and materials from the main library. They offer many of the same kinds of programs as the main library.

Money and Mail

Cities have many banks to handle people's money. The main banks are usually **downtown**. These banks often have **branches** in city **neighborhoods**.

Banks keep people's money safe until they need it.

Workers sort the mail at the post office.

Post offices have a main office downtown, too. They have branch offices in neighborhoods. Letter carriers often deliver the mail on foot because city buildings are so close together.

Other Places in a City

Cities have thousands of important buildings. In the **city hall**, **government** leaders make plans and rules for the city. Cities also have many churches, temples, and other places of worship.

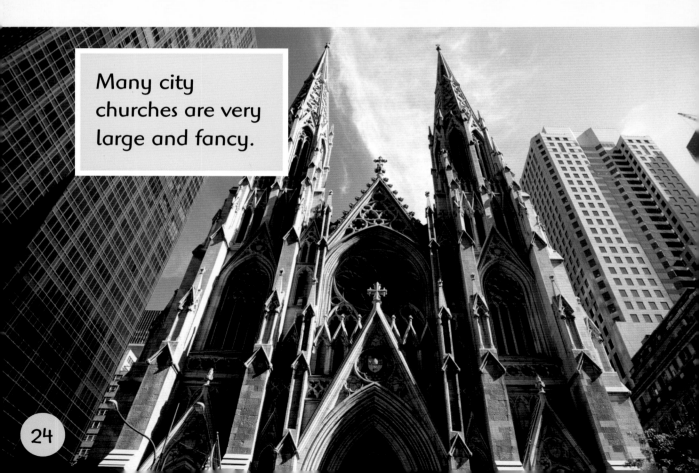

Many city churches are very large and fancy.

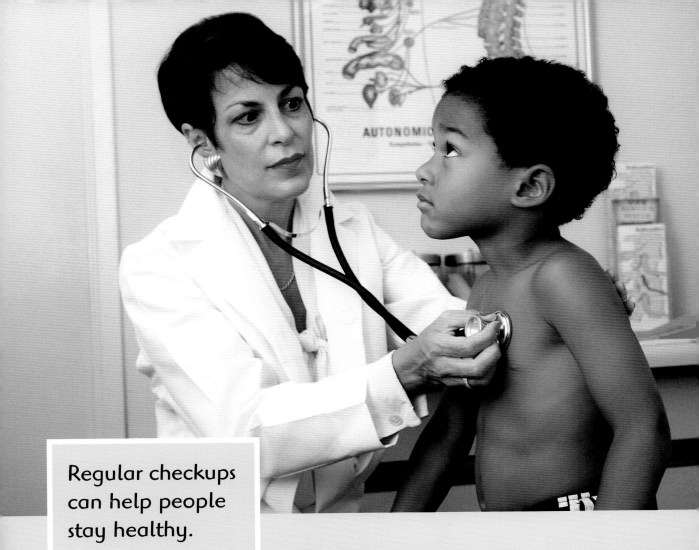

Regular checkups can help people stay healthy.

Cities have many doctors' offices and hospitals. People can get care here when they are sick or hurt. These buildings may be **downtown** or in city **neighborhoods**.

Having Fun

There are lots of fun things to do in a city. Most cities have parks, playgrounds, and gardens for people to enjoy. There are also ball fields, bike paths, and many other places for outdoor activities.

Even **downtown,** people can enjoy the outdoors.

Big cities often have **arenas** where people can watch sports teams play.

Cities have many places to visit. There are **museums** for art, history, and science. There may be **aquariums** and zoos, too. People can also go to theaters to see plays or enjoy music concerts.

The City Comes Together

People in cities collect food to share with those who need it.

A city has many **neighborhoods**, but it is still one big **community**. People work together to help others. They share food, clothing, and other items. They raise money and run special programs for those in need.

People in city neighborhoods also have fun together. They may have parties, parades, and other special events. People share food, music, games, and fun. All these things make cities great places to live.

People in cities celebrate together on special days.

Glossary

ambulance emergency vehicle that carries people who are sick or hurt

aquarium place where water animals and plants are kept and shown

arena large building for sports and other events

ATM bank machine that people use to put in and take out money

branch small part of something bigger

café small restaurant

carpool ride together in one car

city hall building where a city's leaders meet

community group of people who live in one area, or the area where they live

department store large store that sells many different kinds of things

downtown central business section of a city

emergency sudden event that makes you act quickly

farmers' market place where people sell things that were grown or made on farms

government people who make rules for a community, or the rules they make

museum place where special or important items are shown

neighborhood small area of a city or town

patrol travel through an area to keep it safe

subway train that runs underground

town house house that is joined to the houses next to it, usually in a row

vendor person that sells something

More Books to Read

Caseley, Judith. *On the Town: A Community Adventure.* New York: Greenwillow, 2002.

Kalman, Bobbie. *What Is a Community?: from A to Z.* New York: Crabtree Publishing, 2000.

Kehoe, Stasia Ward. *I Live in a City.* New York: PowerKids Press, 2000.

Turnbauer, Lisa. *Living in a City.* Mankato, Minn.: Capstone Press, 2005.

Index